by the same author

Poetry
Salford Road (Penguin)
Song of the City (Collins)
My Granny is a Sumo Wrestler (Collins)
The Fox on the Roundabout (Macmillan)
Can we have our ball back please? (Macmillan)
Collected Poems for Children (Macmillan)

Novels
Saving Grace (Collins)
Rosie No-Name and the Forest of Forgetting (OUP)
The Man with Eyes like Windows (Collins)
The Final Test (Victor Gollancz)
Omelette (Random House)

Gareth Owen was born in Ainsdale, Lancashire. He left school at sixteen and served as a cadet officer in the Merchant Navy for four years. Following an accident in Buenos Aires involving his head and an iron deck, he was invalided out and did various dead-end jobs including market gardening, factory work and bookselling before being accepted as a mature student at Bretton Hall Teacher Training College, Wakefield.

He then taught English and Drama at Downshall Secondary Modern School, Ilford. After four years he became a lecturer at Bordesley College of Education, Birmingham. In Birmingham he began acting, writing and directing at the Crescent Theatre. Three of his plays where broadcast by the BBC, in one of which he took the lead. At the theatre he met a young singer and ended up managing her career: her name was Ruby Turner.

Aged 45 he took early redundancy and since then has lived on his wits, his writing and his broadcasting work. He is the winner of the National *Speak a Poem* Competition which led to him presenting the BBC's long-running *Poetry Please!* for a number of years.

He now lives in Ludlow where he can occasionally be seen as his alter ego, Virg Clenthills, singing self-penned Country songs. For further information consult his website: www.garethowen.com

ISBN: 978-1-300-79241-3

www.publishnation.co.uk

Contents

*

Icarus by Mobile

Selected poems
by
Gareth Owen
*

For Jacquie

The Fox on the Roundabout

A fox upon our roundabout
Watching Saabs and Volvos pass
Like a fully paid-up member
Of our village middle class.

Oldest son at Sandhurst
Daughter at the Sorbonne
Rarely considered the passing years
Or where his life has gone.

Holiday home in Frinton
Thursdays, a hand of Bezique
Treasurer of the Rotary Club
Eighteen holes each week.

Searched for his pipe in his cardi
Broke a buttercup
Wondered should he mow the lawn
Or help with the washing up.

Death of an Old Footballer

He was ready when the whistle blew
Laced up both his boots
Jumped up smiling from the bench
One of life's substitutes.

Raised his arm to the popular end
Flexed the suspect knee
And out of habit showed his studs
To the eternal referee.

Yeah!

Let's face it," Spanner said,
"Fame and money
It's not just a myth, right,
It's got to happen somewhere
And to somebody
So why not us?
And why not now?"
Yeah!
So he borrows seventy quid
Off his nan down Chelmsley Wood
To demo this song of Nigel's
On this little four track in Bob Lamb's in Moseley.
OK, it's a grotty bedroom, yeah,
But it's where UB4O started out
Before they went mega
So there you go.

We laid the rhythm track down first
And though I say it myself
It come over really tasty
With Nige's Fender booming out;
Sort of very 80s, yeah,
But with a touch of Clash in there someplace.

When his turn comes round
Spanner found it hard
Keeping time with the click track;
Pretended like he couldn't give a toss
The way he does

But I could see him sweating cobs,
His fingers fumbling in the strings.
But you have to remember, right,
Apart from Nigel
None of us could play till two months back.
But, like Spanner said,
What's a few bum notes
If the energy's right?
Yeah!
And we all punch the air
And dance around till the floor shakes
And an old bloke downstairs
Starts banging on the ceiling.
You have to laugh, eh!

The vocal, right,
Was down to me.
Like Spanner said
I give it loads of welly.
And I have to say,
Listening to the playback on the cans
With the reverb touching max,
It really come across.
Spanner was bouncing his head
The way he does, you know;
Clicking his fingers.
Yeah!

Well, why be modest, right?
It sounded really great to me.
But then I clock Nige.
He has this look across his face
And I just know he isn't satisfied.
So then I have to do it all again;
And then again!
Ten times!
And still he isn't satisfied
So in the end
Because we're pushed for time
He gets his sister, Karen,
To double up my track -
"Just to thicken out the sound."

Karen! I mean, she's only fifteen!
Goes to ballet classes
And reads books just for the fun of it.
All right, so she can sing in tune
And read music,
But what does she know
About our kind of sound!
This total energy concept
We're trying to generate?
I told Nige what I thought
But he seemed well-pleased
With the track we'd done;
Said the two voices sounded great
And told me not to worry,
Bob and him would fix it in the mix.
Yeah!

When the Local Radio
Played it that Wednesday night
I couldn't believe me ears.
I was nowhere. I mean nowhere.
All you could hear was Karen.
It just wasn't like our sound at all.
Anyway, this Indie Company
Give us a thousand quid advance
And started putting it about.
So thank you very much.
After Peely played it on his show
We got this write-up in the NME
That Spanner got blown up
In case we got some bookings.
Even Radio One picked up on it
And started giving it air time.
Yeah!
We thought, This is it, right,
It's really going to happen.
But all that happened
Was this ginormous silence.
Yeah!
By this time we'd blown the advance
On a C reg Transit.
Was supposed to take us and the gear
To all these gigs we never had.
Spanner went back to fitting tyres
In Bristol Street like he done before.

Then I heard from Nige -
This is on the Thursday, right -
Some A and R man from EMI
Has only signed their Karen up
On a three-year deal.
Yeah!
Last week her first album.
Charted at twenty with a bullet.
Maybe you heard it, right.
No, I didn't think much to it neither
But there you go.

What really pissed me off
Was that after all we'd done
They wouldn't even use our Band
To do the backing track.
Like Spanner said,
There ain't no]ustice
And if there is
Like Fame and Money
It's usually happening
Somewhere out of sight
And in some street
We never walked along.

All the Sad Young Men

Oh, teacher, please, teacher
Don't beat my tiny hand
The answers to your questions
Swarm through my head like sand.
Numbers roll inside my eyes
The words burn holes in me
My brain is locked up like a cage
And they've thrown away the key.

The clerk at the Unemployment
Threw my card in an empty tray
"Got no work for layabouts
Come back another day."
The manager at the shipyard
Kicked me out the door
Didn't like the way I cut my mouth
Didn't like the eyes I wore.

Prime Minister on the TV
Said, "Plenty of work around."
But when I reached the factory
It was bulldozed to the ground.
I talked to this old lady
She was lying by the fence
I wondered why she bled so much
For only fifty pence.
The magistrate polished her glasses
I cried, "Don't send me away.
Don't whisper to each other
Don't stare at me that way."

The courtroom smells of varnish
The law cuts like a knife
There's something being shoved aside
I think it's called my life.

Oh, Mum and Dad, don't send me down
To that cold reformatory
I tried to be someone you could like
But I still came out as me.
Please come up and visit me
The days they pass so slow
Pretend you still both love me
So the other boys won't know.

Asked to see the governor
I didn't like my cell
My poor hands won't stop shaking
My head rings like a bell.
I've carved my name up on the wall
For all the world to see
I read it fifty times a day
To remind myself I'm me.
Oh, doctor who delivered me
Didn't you hear the sound
As you tore me from my mother
And watched my eyes roll round?
Oh, mother, didn't you hear it
As my heart began to knock
The sound of a steel door closing
And a key inside a lock?

The Green Scarf

Alice in her bedroom
Mummy on the stair
Daddy in the stables
Saddling his bay mare.

Alice sees the lady
Hears her silver laugh
Sees the golden hair caught up
In a grass-green scarf.

Alice at the window
Two riders cross the moat
Sees the green scarf knotted
At her daddy's throat.

Alice in her bedroom
Combs her long black hair
Hears hoof beats on the driveway
And weeping on the stair.

Overheard

"Going over Dudley Sunday
have a cup of tea with me nan,"
I overheard the fat man with
I Love Miami
day-gloed across his cap say
at the IKEA checkout counter.
And in that passing moment
behind the simple phrase
I saw a lifetime walking
down an endless street of days.

Gathering in the Days

I saw my grandad late last evening
On a hillside scything hay
Wiped his brow and gazed about him
Gathering in the day.

My grandmother beside the fireplace
Sleeps the afternoons away
Wakes and stirs the dying embers
Gathering in the day.

Heard screams and laughter from the orchard
Saw a boy and girl at play
Watched them turn their heads towards me
Gathering in the day.

And my mother at a window
On some long-forgotten May
Lifts her eyes and smiles upon us
Gathering in the day.

And all the people I remember
Stopped their lives and glanced my way
Shared the selfsame sun an instant
Gathering in the day.

Playing at Dying

She was prepared for dying
Because he'd died before
A hundred times she'd found him
Stiff on the bedroom floor.

He'd fallen out of cupboards
He'd stifled on the mat
He'd drowned in the bath with eyes astare
Struggling like a rat.

He'd slumped to death in the armchair
His hollow eyes remote
He'd choked on the poisoned Horlicks
His hands locked round his throat.

And she but half believing
The game that kept them apart
Begged and cajoled and exhorted
Till her fingers found his heart.

"It's only a game," he'd told her.
"You know I only pretend."
So she waited by the gravestone
For the game to end.

Siesta

Each day at this same hour
He comes to her;
His lady of the afternoons.
Behind closed lids she hears the whispering
  brush-strokes
Gathering in the light, the windows and her
sleeping form.
Her countenance is often in his dreams
But these are things not spoken of.
Outside the room where all this happens ,
In a splash of sunlight by the kitchen door
A maid trades amorous gossip with the gardener's
boy
While shelling peas into her wide-spread lap;
A petal falls, someone puts out washing;
And in the orchard among oranges
Her husband, whose idea it was,
Tends his bees, his face inside a net.
"I'm working on your mouth," the painter tells
her.
She does not know his Christian name.
Her shut lids tremble.]ust so
She used to close her eyes in childhood
 Feigning sleep or death;
Then open them in sudden laughter
To see her father's great moon - face
Filling the everywhere;

Then later he was further off.
And later still an absence,
Like a place she took her heart to ache in.
Remembering this, she feels herself
Absorbed into the room
And in the darkness there,
Beyond the limits of herself,
Senses the painter with his canvas gone away
And lines of curious, reverential strangers
Filing past the open door
To gaze on her:
Like one already dead.

The Phantom of the Lake

Last night I rose up from my bed
And walked beside the lake
I saw the pale moon ride the sky
Heard the cold waves break.

A girl stood at my window sill
Her face gleamed mournfully
A fearful cry rose in her throat
As she turned away from me.

And I wondered if they told her
In the morning by that shore
Of the girl who one day drowned there
A hundred years before.

Street

In the street where I was born
Strangers come and go
Returning after thirty years
There's no one that I know.

Intruders squatting in my home
It's more than I can bear
And beyond the edges of my life
It's happening everywhere.

Kiss and Tell

Squatting in the sunlit gravel
Where the spell first struck
Frogprince sighed a regal, philosophic sigh.
"Ho hum. Well there we are," he murmured,
Deciding then and there
That sang-froid was the order of the day.
Besides, hadn't they warned him countless times
How any untoward excitement
Might one day dam for ever
The silted arteries of his princely heart.
And on balance, he thought to himself,
Taking the long view,
The rough with the smooth -
Didn't being a live frog
Have it hands down any day of the week
Over being a dead prince.
He thought it did.
Besides, being always up to speed
With all the latest fairy tales,
He knew it only required
One lovelorn princess passing by
To plant that magic juicy one
Upon his froggy lips
And, Hey Sahazzam!
Farewell froggydom;
Hello Princey once again

Not to speak of Happy Ever After;
Children laughing on the sunlit lawn
And the gleaming Testa Rossa

Crouching on the Royal Drive.
So, weighing all things up
Frogprince hunched smiling on his lily pad
Contentedly awaiting his lovely saviour
To dance across the dew
And change his life.

Back at the palace though
Times were hard:
The Palace ballroom and the Counting House
Had both sprung leaks;
The peasantry was muttering and reading books;
And down at the drawbridge,
Where talk was of the Princess
And her body piercing,
Four and twenty bailiffs
Gathered like hunchbacked crows.

Frogprince, of course, knew nought of this.
So when he saw his princess
Prancing pondwards through the moonlight
He fondly reflected,
"Ho hum it's transformation time,"
And puckered up.
But alas the golden butterflies
That danced across his lips
Were all too much for him.
The frail paper of his heart
Ripped into tatters
And back he fell with a froggy plop
Into the pond
And croaked.

Hardly had the ripples settled
Before the Princess,
Swallowing her disappointment
And a green chartreuse,
Was back in the Palace Press Room
Hammering out her exclusive to the world:

Stolen Pond side Date
Of Love Tryst Princess
And Amphibian Lover
Ends in Tragic Death Kiss!

Girl from a Train

We stopped by a cornfield
Near Shrewsbury
A girl in a sun hat
Smiled at me.

Then I was seven
Now sixty-two
Wherever you are
I remember you.

Schoolgirl on a Train

When the girl
I'd never seen before
Who wore the tie
And scarlet uniform
Of the Catholic School
And whose dark eyes
Had almost stopped
The traffic of my fifteen-year-old blood,
Rose to leave the train
At the station after the golf course
I prayed she'd leave behind
The magazine she read so avidly
So I could read
The selfsame words her eyes had read
And whisper to myself
She read that
She read that
She read that.

Days at School

Like every day
I open our front door.
Against the creosote fence,
Above the clustering pansies
The roses glow dull red;
And further off
Beyond the maple
And the overgrown canal
The orphan hill
That has no name
Rises to the blue.
Like every morning
I stand in the lay-by
In Penthryn Lane
Waiting for the bus.

Brakes squeal.
Ann, the driver, wears a boiler suit
And works at Revill's garage in the town.
"Remind your mum
To leave me half a dozen eggs,"
She shouts her eyes upon the road ahead.
Because it's]une and hot today
I sit with Kelly at the back
Beside an open window.
She's not my best friend
But you can always talk to her.

The wind that's blown across the Irish sea
And half the breadth of Wales
Before rustling our homework books
And my brown hair
Smells hot today of grass and tar.
Today we're up to Air and Light
In our Jam Jar Science Books.
Later we'll climb on the roof
To drop paper parachutes
On to the playing fields below.
Around the iron gates
The children shout and stare
As we get off the bus.

Next September I'll be at the High School
And someone else
Will sit in my place by the window.
There are stars that die each minute
Before their light comes down to us.
The bell rings
And we crowd shouting
Towards the shadows and the open door.

Envelopes and Letters

She felt the shock of love
Was like that moment in a dream
When the whole earth opens up on emptiness
And the falling was for ever
And for ever.
And walking here and there
Down thronging corridors
Among the desks and chairs
She threaded through the other girls
Leaving her silence in the air
Like a scented wake to occupy the space.
And sitting at her desk in History
All unbeckoned, the thought came in:
That she was like an envelope
That bore nor name nor destination;
And what she felt, was like a letter
The boy had scrawled his name and life upon.
She thought this when the teacher
Questioned her about the dream she occupied
Saying only
Nothing, Miss, nothing,
It's nothing.

Crush

In the second term of the fifth year,
That month we won the Final
Of the Intermediate Cup
And the snow came late
Covering all the playing fields
And heaping up against the Sports Hall,
I came a pearler off my bike
Delivering the *Daily Post*
In Abercrombie Road.
And as I sat there
Deciding if I was alive or dead
This dark-haired girl in a red coat
Jumped off the fifteen bus
And asked me if I was all right.
And alive or dead was not a question any more
Because I've seen this girl before
On Saturdays in Rushworth's
Playing records in a booth
With Pete Almond's sister's cousin
Who's in her class at school
And says she'll fix me up with her
If I'm that desperate.
And Oh, I am, I am that desperate
Because there is no hope
And I am drowning
In those eyes of hers
Those dark grey eyes
That nail my aching heart
And tongue for ever down.

And is this me
My face on fire
Looping the oily chain back on
With streaked and trembling hands
Walking my buckled bike
Back up the road away from her
Cursing my coward heart
For all those witty things
I know I could have said
But never did?

And is this me
Writing my name and hers together
With an equals in between
In the unbroken snow
Of empty Hesketh Park?
Making a spell against the thaw
They say is bound to come.

Lovesick

I am a schoolgirl sick with love
I mope and gaze at the moon
I don't know who the boy is yet
I hope I meet him soon.

The Gift

He's waiting for me when I wake
In the shadows on the stair
In the classroom and the yard
He's waiting for me everywhere.

He gives me blows and lashing words
I give him silence and my cries
And from this bargain something grows
A twisted friendship made of lies.

And there is nowhere I can hide
For even when we're miles apart
He haunts the pillow where I lie
Nursing the bruises of my heart.

And when they ask me for his name
My tongue's a stone, my eye a tear
But in my skull I hear him cry,
"Your name is Victim, mine is Fear!"

And after, though he'd left that place
The fear he'd planted in me grew
So now I'm standing on the stair
To pass it on to someone new.

Bird

Something fluttered about my heart
Like a bird caught in a snare
I blame the girl on the fourteen bus
It was she who put it there.

Unemployable

'I usth thu workth in the thircusth,'
he said
Between the intermittent showers that
emerged from his mouth.
'Oh,' I said, 'what did you do?'
'I usth thu catcth bulleth in my theeth.'

An Attempt at the Shortest Poem in the World

Already
This is too long.

Country Singer's Lament

I made a million singing love songs
Got two wives chasing me,
They live in Hope and Bitterness
I live in Tennessee.

Old Boys' Register

Allendale and Belton and Belvedere and Blunt
Hildyard and Jackson and Johnson and Lunt
Mildwood and Mowbray and Naysmith and Knight
Sineheart and Tildon and Unstead and White.
And Wylde?

Allendale swotted and always came first
Belton had boils that never burst
Belvedere was good at Art
Blunt used to fart.
And Wylde?

Hildyard was sharp and wore loud ties
Jackson took pleasure in torturing flies
Johnson bragged about the girls he'd had
Lunt was mad.
But Wylde?

Mildwood tried to hold your hand
Mowbray buried him in the sand
Naysmith was a useful bat
Knight was fat.
But Wylde?

Sinehart said he didn't care
Tildon who was never there
Unstead sang the latest hits
White had fits.
Was Wylde the one who smiled to himself?

And now:
Allendale runs his father's store
Belton apparently studied law
Belvedere's a diplomat in Spain
Blunt's insane.
Did Wylde sit by the Window?

Hildyard is something in the States
Jackson sells brooms round housing estates
Johnson married a wealthy bride
Lunt died.
But Wylde?

Mildwood went to teach abroad
Mowbray is a rep with Ford
Naysmith wandered far and wide
Knight tried.
/\nd Wylde?

Sineheart surprised us by flying high
Tildon's researching for ICI
Unstead demos enamel sinks
White drinks.
And Wylde took a shotgun and blew out the brains of his three
children.

Dad

Two days before he died
My sister made a bed for him
In what they called his living room.
Too busy chasing every breath by now
The irony passed him by.
On the TV in the corner
Two ageing gunslingers
Challenged each other
To one last shoot-out
Before a paying audience
In the sand-strewn bullring.
"Winner takes all," snarled Kirk,
But what the winner takes, I thought,
Is what we all of us will get
If we hang around unchallenged long enough.
They never said that in those
Happy Ever After films
We once were nourished on;
That always faded in impassioned kisses.
But after in the streets outside,
Hurrying homewards to our several lives,
We soon found out, that After is not for Ever;
That even star-kissed lips
Dissolve to dust in Time.

Westerns he'd always liked;
But this last one outlived him
So he never saw the final
Thundering shoot-out in the sun,
Nor heard the diapason swell

Above the closing titles
And the last dissolve.

Punctilious to the last,
Sensing an appointment to be kept,
He wound his watch a final time;
Told Anne he loved her,
Then composed himself until
The erratic knocking in his wrist
Gave up the ghost for good.

Someone opened a window
For his fleeing soul.
And across the hills
The great and endless night
Came pouring in from everywhere.

Never be Another Dixie

Ten, I must have been
When my dad took me to my first game.
Maybe a birthday, I don't know.
Walking the long walk to the ground
From Bankhall Station,
Each fifty yard or so
His dicky lungs gave out
And he would have to rest
Slumping, hunched upon some stranger's wall;
Inhaling from his pump
Each desperate, shallow breath.
At ten I was embarrassed
Wished he'd get on with it
For fear we missed the kick off.

The ground was like a huge liner
Surprised to be moored
Amongst the huddled, meagre houses.
He saw me to the Boys' Pen
While he stood with the swaying crowd
Behind the goal at Gwladys Street.
Can't remember much about the game
Somebody called McKnight scored:
A diving header at the near post.
One-one I think it ended up.
Once I caught a glimpse of him
Struggling amongst the waving arms
To get the borrowed breath into his lungs.

On the train home I read the programme
Or watched suburban houses
And the golf links flashing by
As he talked endlessly
About the heroes of his youth:
Jimmy Dunn and Critchley
Warney Cresswell, Dixie Dean.
'Never be another like Dixie,'
He said, his eyes on something
Further off than I could understand.
I wasn't listening really
I never did.

And then the other day
I bought a video: *The Everton Story.*
The kind of thing fanatics buy
Who have a taste for history and the game.
And there suddenly, grainy on the screen,
Was the great man in his prime;
William Ralph Dean Esquire in black and white;
Burly and menacing, levering himself on air
To nod another past some jersied, hapless keeper.
Then, something in the background caught my eye:
A small, smudged figure laughing in the crowd
The right hand raised in exaltation
As his clear breath danced on the air,
Rising up from uncongested lungs
Crying 'Goal' to the dark sky
As the headed ball crossed the line
And the white net billowed.

Hamlet

Well, he had something of your height,
Compact, I'd say, but by no means slight;
Approachable, certainly, although patrician
But with something dangerous in his disposition:
A passion wedded to urbanity,
A kind of elegant barbarity
That many others found attractive.
An intellect that was speculative
Rather than analytic. Fond of the stage
And skilful with the foils as any of his age.
Sat a horse well, knew how to dress,
Drank a little, swore, but never to excess —
At least not that I heard tell,
But then I never knew him quite as well
As many you could ask. A student tends
To gravitate to exclusive groups of friends
And so it was with me. The last
I saw of him was when his carriage passed
My college window. He had to leave
Quite suddenly for Elsinore:
I never quite found out what for;
Trouble in the family I believe.

The Good Handyman's Guide to Fantasy

Now in those far off days
When Gutter Drip the Dragon Slayer
Still walked the harsh land
Of Downpipe Overlap Bolted Together,
Which lay between the mountain of
Spindlewasher
And the mighty ocean of Upper Sash,
Word came wind-borne
From the Kingdom of that greatest of Lords,
Whom men call, Architrave Door Sag:
That in the night when no stars shone
The great dragon, Screed Batten Wall Render,
He of the mitred corners and the bare-faced tenon,
Bearing on his back his master
That most treacherous necromancer,
Ridge Tile Slaters Ripper,
Took up the sleeping forms
Of Architrave Door Sag's two daughters:
Bracket For Half Round Guttering,
Of whose beauty
The like has not been seen
Since the world first breathed,
And her younger sister,
Inspection Trap Screw Plunger.
And these two maids the monster bore from
thence
Upon the spiny ridges of his dragon back
To that shadowy, fearful cavern
That lies between the peaks
Of Rebate Hanger Hinge

Which Ridge Tile Slaters Ripper
Called his home.

Now when Architrave Door sag
Heard these fateful tidings
He was sore peeved
And fell forthwith into a state
Of frittering indecisiveness
And weeping called out to his people saying:
"Listen my people, for it is I
Architrave Door Sag that speaks onto you."
And his people replied with one great voice,
"We know that already."
And Architrave Door Sag
Drew from its stone scabbard
The great and shimmering blade
That men call Mantelpiece Surround.
And waving it thrice
About his grey and grizzled locks
Raised up his mighty voice once more and said:
"Which one of you now, O my warriors,
Will venture forth alone
To the land of Rebate Hanger Hinge
And challenge there in battle onto death
Screed Batten Wall Render
And his master, the necromancer,
Ridge Tile Slaters Ripper
Under the blood red sky of
Downpipe Overlap Bolted Together
And bring back to my bosom
My two fair daughters:
Bracket For Half Round Guttering

And my youngest, my beloved
Inspection Trap Screw Plunger
Whose eyes are of the hue
Of Hessian Webbing Rubber.
Who will do this?"
And when they heard this tearful plea
Each man assembled there stepped forth
And with one great voice cried out:
"Him! Him!"

Now when he heard this
Lord Architrave Door Sag
Turned to his most faithful servant,
Hose Pipe Wire Bending
And in a whisper,
So that his voice was like on to
Wind that hath long lain trapped,
Said: "Hose Pipe Wire Bending
Most loyal of Men
Seek you out the great warrior,
Gutter Drip Dragon Slayer
And charge him with this task.
And tell him for reward
He shall have as bride
The virgin hand
Of whomsoever of my daughters
Shall please him best.
Tell him this."

Ten long and bitter years elapsed
'Ere Hose Pipe Wire Bending,
His hair now white with toil and pain,
Limped nigh to death
Back to the castle of Architrave Door Sag.
But 'ere yet one word of what he knew
Could quit those ancient wrinkled lips
He waved a paper in the air
And groaning fell from off his steed
Where Yeoman Death, who waits upon us all,
Bore him swift away
To that far land men call
Stop Cock.

And Architrave Door Sag
Plucked up the paper that erstwhile
Fell from Hose Pipe Wire Bending's hand
And read aloud the fateful words
That Gutter Drip had written there:

Sorry, I'm not available at the moment
Please leave your name and message
And I'll get back to you
As soon as possible
Thank you.

Silent Poem

(4' 33" is the title of a piece for any instrument
by John Cage. It consists of the performer sitting
in silence for the stipulated time.)

Please listen carefully:
In what follows
The terms *poem* and *silence*
Shall be taken to be synonymous and
   interchangeable.
The silences we shall be concerned with
Shall be those silences we shall be concerned with
And none other.
Please be on the alert for imitations.
For what we are gathered here to observe
Is an absence; a non existence.
I repeat non existence.
It is important therefore
That you remain seated.
Do not, I repeat, not leave the room.
Were we all to do so
There would be nobody here
To observe the existence of this non existence.
I cannot impress upon you too seriously
How grave such a case would be.
If however your departure proves unavoidable
Please do so with the minimum of fuss.
To facilitate this

Please observe now your nearest exit point,
Plan your route in advance,
Move silently. Walk, don't run.

The words.
Between the silences will be words.
The words however are not the poem.
They exist merely to draw our attention to the
    Silence/poem.
Those at the beginning
Indicate the imminence of the silence.
Those at the end
Indicate that the silence is concluded.

Should you, by some chance,
Hear silences other than those
With which we are concerned
There is no cause for agitation.
You are undergoing a species of religious
experience
Commonly known as, not hearing voices.
]oan of Arc did not suffer from this.
Thank you for your attention
When all is ready I shall begin.

I'm sorry that was not the poem.
I repeat not the poem.
That silence was mistaken.
Those of you who believe it was a poem
Erase it from your memory.

Here is the poem.

Someone made a sound.
The silence could not make itself heard.
I shall therefore read the poem again.

Here is an encore.

Here is the poem backwards.

This is the poem read more slowly.

Here is the poem sideways.

Here is the poem translated into Welsh.

This time all join in the chorus.

You may take this poem home with you
When you are feeling tired
Recite it to yourself thus:

It can be obtained
On any wave of your radio.
Simply turn the on/off switch
To the *off* position.

There it was again.
If you should choose
To recite it in public
Please pay your royalties promptly.
On this occasion as you listen
Analyse the rhyme scheme.

Finally here is the poem once more
In its original form.

Aaaaaaaaaaaaagh!
Do not be alarmed
That was not the poem expressing pain.
Silence is of its nature silent
And suffers without complaint.
This has its dangers
For like a body which registers no pain
It may extinguish itself unobserved.
Remember that
The next time you break it.

The Mother

Erich.
That is my boy there
My son, in the second lane.
There you see.
Well, you would not know from looking
Now he is twenty five years of age.
He is more like his father than me.
But still I think of him as a boy.
Am I proud?
Ah yes naturlich
Proud as any mother would be.
But also I feel something
That you might call sadness.
So many people here!
So large a stadium
That the Fuehrer has built for us!
So many important people!
And my son there, so small
You know, so small.
And he must carry all this;
For Germany, for the Fuehrer;
For all these people.
It should not be eh.
People should not live through others.
It will destroy him perhaps.
So small you see.
But I am a mother
I do not see what the rest of them see,
No.

For them he is a runner,
Oh yes, better than most;
Perhaps the best in the world.
But it does not matter.
They see only the outside;
The speed, the strength, the cruelty-
Yes cruelty.
For to wish so much to be the first
There must be a kind of cruelty there.
But I see him as a boy still,
As he once was,
Sickly you know
And always missing school.
It was the doctor said he should run,
And when he ran
He ran faster than the wind.
Yes the wind.
It was a gift;
Something inside him.
He loved to run.
'Mutti,' he shouted to me,
'Look how I run!'
He feels so light on his feet sometimes
That he tells me almost he can fly.
So, when I see him, there is this sadness.
I don't know why it comes to me
Or where it comes from
But always it is there;
Proud and at the same time sad.
That's how it is.
And also, a kind of fear;
Something breathing beneath my heart

That fears for all of us;
Almost something burning.
And then I see him,
My little boy,
Like a photograph in black and white;
We stand so. Still, he and I.
Frozen so, you see.
I am coming from the kitchen
Of our first house in Bavaria,
Coming from the kitchen
With some ashes in a bucket.
And the ashes are still red,
Still smouldering.
And the smell it has. Pah!
The sun is shining and it is May.
Suddenly he comes from the garden to me
Wearing glasses, for his eyes were bad then.
He is seven, almost eight.
In his right hand is a sword
His father had from the war.
He sees me and stops.
And we look at one another,
Very still. So.
As he looks, he smiles.
This smile I cannot describe;
This look on his young face.
But what this smile says to me,
What it says is;
- Mother I know;
I know more than you understand.

And what I am thinking
There in the sunshine of May
With the ashes burning bitter in my hand,
What I am thinking is,
That there are things here about him
That I will never understand.
And it is as though,
While this is happening -
That I am looking back on it,
Staring back with my mind
The ashes burning in the sunshine
The sword in his hand
And his face smiling-
And I am thinking:
This is why he runs.
This is why we all run.

*Note: This poem was part of a verse play commissioned by BBC radio. It was based on the 1936 Berlin Olympic Games in which the black American athlete, much to the chagrin of Adolf Hitler, won four gold medals.
I supposed the Speaker to be the mother of one of the German athletes.*

Home Thoughts from Abroad 2

I'm driving down the 'Frisco turnpike
Through blazing California sun
But in my mind I'm with the faithful
Behind the goal at Goodison.

At 'Joey's Diner', Fifth and Sunset
Cicadas hymn the shimmering heat
While December echoes with the singing there
Soaring up from Gwladys Street.

Make the call from my motel room
Surf rolls in beneath the sun
"Dad, it's me from Santa Barbara
Tell me how the Blues got on."

Saint Domingo's

And didn't the Reverend preach me into a snooze
That never-ending drizzle of a Sunday.
The gas lights on for the dark outside
And the old tobacco smell
Filling my nose off Dad's best suit.
The theme of it's clean gone from me:
Something about women and the worth of rubies.
And I smiled at pretty Alice Parks
Who sat demure among the choristers.

After the final prayer I meant to walk
With her down St Domingo Grove
But found her, arm in arm with some new chap
Her brother says she's sweet on fit to bust.
I watched them strolling off, then made my way
Through Stanley Park, not marking where I went,
Until I came on ten jovial-seeming chaps
Playing at football beside the Stanley House.
Good fellows all. They asked me to join in
And though I'd hardly played the game before
I kicked and tackled like a thing possessed
Until the thought of Alice Parks was gone from me.

At dusk they asked me back to play again.
And I think, you know, perhaps I will.
At twenty-one I know I'm starting late
But had a sense of something new beginning
On rain-soaked Stanley Park in 1878.

(*The first Everton team was formed at the St
Domingo Congregational Chapel, Liverpool in
1878.)

Football Manager at Prayer

Here we are again, Lord
Last home game of the season
Needing that precious point
To save us from the drop.
A point is all I'm asking Lord;
One measly, rotten point.
Not too much to ask is it?
Not after the luck we've had.
From the start things never broke our way:
That sending off, first game at Sunderland;
The whistle-happy ref at White Hart Lane;
The easy chances that we never put away;
Penalties ballooned into the stand
And the woodwork always playing for them.
And injuries! Lord, the injuries!
The treatment room was like the ward at Casualty.
And now the crowd is getting on my back:
Spraying the car and the Birkdale house
With filthy things you wouldn't credit.
Even our Tracy, who's only five,
Is getting stick from kids at school.
What kind of money can compensate for that?
You tell me. Why bother I say.
Load of other ways to earn my crust
With only half the grief.
Myra's been on at me for ages
To get the kitchen and the patio fixed.
Still got my City and Guilds;
Plumbing's not a bad trade;
Steady, you know, and the money's fair.

At least you don't get thirty thousand fans
Screaming for your blood if a tap starts dripping.
Old ticker's giving me gyp again and all.
The wife's been on to me ages to see the Quack.
But where's the time I say.
In a hectic season like we've just had;
Are twenty two prima donnas
Kicking a bag of wind about
Worth dying for? I don't think so.
Still – If we could just scratch a draw today;
Buy in a player or two!
Fresh start next season.
No knowing what we might not do.

The Classic Cinema Club

We gather here by candle light
To gaze on shadows. Odd pastime this:
Surrendering our diverse selves
To occupy a dream that's not our own.
Strange too, that what is nothing really
But a mote-filled spear of light
That plays upon this simple, stretched white sheet
Should thus awake our passive hearts
To laughter, to regret and pain.
And these, whose travails we now revisit here:
Gary Cooper, Buster Keaton, Greta Garbo, Fred Astaire
Somehow become familiars, whose myriad fictive lives
We've grown to know as well as our own flesh:
Gloria Swanson, Orson Welles, Arletty, Jean Gabin.
And with this, a sense of all those other selves
Who we once were, comes seeping back to us
Across the years; of how, we slumped
In plush back rows of smoke-filled palaces,
Our eyes raised to the kissing stars up on the screen,
Urging our timid, adolescent arms to rise and fold
About the enticing but forbidding waists of girls
Whose names we now can scarce recall.
Now, here they are once more, those long, cold stars;
Larger than life and younger here than we shall ever be:
Lana Turner, Jimmy Stewart, Judy Garland, Cary Grant.
And we rise up and meet them on some central ground:
The brave ones, the comic, the beautiful and the sad.
And all we've ever been to one another rises up
Like distant memories we somehow almost had.

Saturday Night at the Bethlehem Arms

Very quiet really for a Saturday.
Just the old couple come to visit relations
Who took the double room above the yard
And were both of them in bed by half- past nine.
Left me with that other one, the stranger.
Sat like he was set till Doomsday at the corner of the bar
Sipping small beer dead slow and keeping mum;
Those beady, tax-collector's eyes of his
On my reflection in the glass behind the bar
Watching me, watching me.
And when he did get round to saying something
His talk was like those lines of gossamer
That fishermen send whispering across the water
To lure and hook unwary fish.
I'm no fish. Not my type.
And anyway I'd been on the go since five.
Dead beat I was.
Some of us have a bed to go to, I thought to myself.
I was just about to call Time
When the knock came at the door.
At first I was for turning them away:
We only have two rooms see and both of them were
taken.
But something desperate in the woman's eyes
Made me think again and I told them,
They could rough it in the barn
If they didn't mind the cows and mules for company.

I know, I know. Soft, that's me.
I yawned; locked up; turned out the lights;
Rinsed my hands to lose the smell of beer;
Went up to bed.
A day like any other.
That's how it is.
Nothing much ever happens here.

The Poet

The morning sky was flocked with words
Flying high like singing birds
He fed them breath and light and bread
And now they're on this page instead.

.

Jack in the Sky

Jack popped his head through a door in the sky
Hopped down Memory Street
Raised his hat to the smiling world
And the friends he chanced to meet.

He danced in the eye of the afternoon
Smiled at all he saw
While puss on the sun–warmed doorstep purred
And licked her folded paw.

Jane on a swing in the garden green
Her yellow hair flowed free
Smiled at the ghost of brother Jack
That only she could see.

.

Shadowplay

Ann runs down the garden path
As fast as she knows how
Out to the daisy-freckled lawn
She calls the Here and Now.
'Look,' she says, 'look at my shadow
How it spreads so dark and tall.
But when I lie flat with my face in the grass
There's no shadow of me at all.'
Mummy wears lilies pressed to her breast
The car is long and black
'Look at the game I'm playing,' says Ann,
'It's called, Pushing the Shadows Back.'

The Letter

Robin goes walking where the strange things are
Down through the garden but not too far.
Robin leaves a letter on the greenhouse shelf
Leaves a long letter addressed to himself.

Robin in the playground but no on wants to play
So he walks down the garden at the end of the day,
Down through the garden where the world shines green
To see in the greenhouse if the postman's been.

Stranger in the House

I have entered the Wrong house again!
Creeping from room to room I wonder
Where are my carpets and my chairs;
My family photographs, my books;
My watercolours done by hand?
Even the smell is different.
A strange dog bounds panting down the stairs
And slobbers his affection on my hand.
And then these children
I have never seen before
Call me their father;
Clutch my hand and laughing
Crawl upon my knee.
And who is this tall woman
Who greets me with a kiss
Laying cool hands upon my face
And whispering in my ear
Sweet names I've never heard before?
And when alone at last
I face my bedroom glass
Some shifty, callow counterfeit
Stares back at my discomfiture.
No, I have certainly entered
The wrong house again.
Tomorrow something must be done.
But the habits of a lifetime-
Are hard to break.

Icarus

Icarus spat out by sun
As fly from cat's mouth
Fell through dimensions of eternity
Danced the idiot's dance
Down broken rungs of sky
Discharged his senses on the stars
The screaming was outside himself
Ears baring teeth
Tore up his scalp
His eyes hooked out by windy claws
Crawled on his face.
The sea crashed up
With scales of fire
Earth was upside down
Death's hand wrenching his hair
Sent tremors and blood spinning
Out to the world's edge
World rolled in his bowels
Inside was out
Felt the sea
Like spikes of rock
Crack his bones
Spring his ribs
Spread his lungs on red water
His nature
Cracked by air and sea
Buoyed belly up
Fell open
Like the secret of a flower

Icarus by Mobile

Daddy, Daddy is that you?
Listen I don't have much time OK
But I wanted to say, right
It's back to the drawing board, Daddy
The whole contraption is a no no.
The wings?
No, the wings worked fine
Couldn't fault the wings in any way
The wings were ace
And your calculations on the stresses
Re wind and feathers
Spot on!
Likewise the pinion tolerances
And remember that flap factor
That gave us both such sleepless nights
Let me tell you
Those flaps worked like a dream
But Daddy
Oh, Daddy
How could you forget the sun!
You told me?
What is this 'I told you'!
I don't have much time
So listen OK
We're talking equations here
Just let me spell it out for you:
Solar heat + bees' wax + ambition =
Total Meltdown and I mean total
Which equals to put it simply
Your boy Icarus on collision course

With something called the Earth.
Daddy, I don't have much time
Let me give you my co-ordinates
For the pick-up
OK stretch of headland and a bay
Visibility good outlook calm. And hey
Am I lucky or am I lucky!
There's a galleon anchored near the shore
Looks like Icarus
Is in for an early pick-up this fine morning.
And over there some poor old farmer's
Ploughing through a field of stones
And here's an old boy with a fishing pole and
Listen, Daddy
Would you believe
Some guy just out of frame
Is painting the whole thing.
And now I'm waving, Daddy, waving
Any minute now they'll all look up and
So listen, Daddy, I don't have much time
I'm going to start screaming soon OK?
Can you still hear me?
I don't have much
Daddy, I just wanted to ask
You know
About my mum
Was she
Listen Daddy
I don't have much time
I

Hound Dog and Heartbreak

Must've been in me pram
When I heard them all first time round:
Hound Dog and *Mystery Train,*
Heartbreak Hotel
And *Blue Moon of Kentucky.*
So you might say the King was in my blood.
At eight I'd sing along to the Dansette
Hitting the poses for the bedroom mirror
The legs going haywire;
Strumming the broken racket.
And the old fella screaming up the stairs,
"Shut up yer bleeding row for God's sake."

At fourteen I started shaving,
Thickened out the sideburns with Mam's pencil
Brylcreamed the pompadour
And locked the sneer in permanent
With a paperclip by night.
But things really started to take off
When I come equal second, highly commended
In the *Elvisly Yours Look Alike Contest*;
Three girls screamed and made me
Autograph their arms with lipstick
And I got to kiss Tina behind *The Grapes*
That never-to-be-forgotten October night.

It was all for the King
But I felt this tide of fame
Beckoning to me from afar.

On Jan 8th '69, His birthday,
I changed my name to you-know-what by deed
poll
And me and Tina starts shacking up.
I was working in accounts
For Metal Box back then.
Not what He'd have done I know
But every penny I could save
Was all for Elvis and the Dream.
It started with the white karate suits
The silk cloak and the diamantés.
Then we had the pillars
Erected out the front
And the whole downstairs
Done out like Graceland.
The place was a shrine.
People came from miles
To Capon Road to stand and stare
And *Midlands Today* come down
And did this interview
With me in all the gear. Magic!
Worked all the hours God sent me
To make the payments on the nose
The transplant and the lips.
Tina couldn't stand it in the end:
"I don't know who I'm sleeping with no more."
She screamed and took off for her mum's
Taking little Elvis with her.
She didn't understand,
Women don't, do they?

I was gutted something rotten
But at least I understood
What He'd gone through
When that Priscilla walked out on him.
I don't want to talk about
What happened in '77.
I tell you it near finished me.

Don't open the door to nobody no more
Only go out to pick the giro up.
To help the swelling in me legs
I sit in the bath for hours some nights
Eating cream cakes and supping lager.
The plug hole's clogged with hair
And the silence is something else.
Wednesday I put an advert in the Mail,
Old Hound Dog is Lonesome Tonight!
At the Heartbreak Hotel.
Vacancies.
Call any time.

Blind Date

You are who I think you are, aren't you?
I thought you were
You had that look
Pick you out a mile.
Bucks Fizz'll do me fine.
Look, you won't mind will you
If I get something off my chest?
Well, I don't want you to take this personally
But I don't think much of men.
If you'd known my ex
You'd feel the same.
No, not hate exactly
He didn't have the character
To be someone you could hate -
I resented that in him -
No, it was just that he was
A slimy, spineless, two-timing bastard
Who thought I was too stupid
To know what was going on
Between him and that Linda
Whatsername down in Graphics.
Apart from that he was perfect.
Even had the cheek to introduce me to her
At the staff and wives shindig that Christmas.
I felt sorry for her really.
Well, you'd feel sorry for anybody
Who thought my Barry was wonderful.
I thought it would fizzle out
But it didn't. So in the end
I did my big confrontation bit.

'Course, he puts on this innocent
Who, me? Look.
But his eyes were all over the place.
Yes, I'll have another, thanks.
Does it bother you if I smoke?
It does some.
What was I saying?
Oh yes, like I said
He tried to deny it,
Said it had been Linda's fault
She'd been all over him from the start,
Wouldn't leave him alone
Or take no for an answer.
I was the only one he really loved,
I had to believe him.
Then he starts crying. Real tears!
He thought that would make it all right.
Pathetic! "What about me, Barry?" I said,
"What about my tears?"
What do men know about crying?
Where weeping's concerned
I'm the world's expert.
He said it was all over between them
I told him, it had better be
Or he wouldn't see the house,
The BMW or the kids again.
That really put the frighteners on him.
So, we were all right for a bit.
I got this promotion at Jacksons:
Area Sales, Roller Blinds.
It's very interesting really.
What do you do?

Oh, I see that must be nice.
Anyway, three months after all this
He comes to me with this sad story
How Linda's three months gone
By this spotty Herbert in Dispatch
Who's still wet behind the ears
And everywhere else by all accounts.
He said, he just felt sorry for her
She being just eighteen and everything;
Her mum and dad were Jehovah's Witnesses
And were going to chuck her out.
Couldn't we put her up for a few months?
Just till everything quietened down.
I said to him straight
I said: "Barry, tell me the truth.
It is all over with you and her isn't it?"
He said: "What sort of man d'you think I am?
D'you think I'd lie to you?"
I didn't answer that.
Am I talking too much?
Just stop me if I do.
Anyway, like a fool, I let her stay.
That Friday she moved in with us
And we gave her the room in the back.
Got on all right too I must say.
She was good with Philippa and Mark.
It was really nice as well
Having another woman around the place.
She even started decorating the bedrooms.

Then one afternoon
I had this call from Head Office.
Someone had let them down
At the last minute
Could I go and demo these New Age roller blinds
At the Broad Street Conference Centre?
I'd only got as far as Harborne
When I suddenly realised
I'd left the costings and some samples
In the boot of Barry's car.
They can't have heard the Astra in the drive
Frankly, I'm not surprised the noise she was
making.
They heard the door though.
I heard this desperate whispering
And rustling in our room.
When I went up they'd tried to cover up the bed;
Said they were decorating.
I don't know if I cried.
I didn't want to in front of her.
You know what really hurt?
She was even wearing that kimono
Barry bought at Rackhams for our tenth.
I just walked out.
Went to my mum and dad's;
Something cracked inside me.
For a year I didn't go out of the house;
I didn't see the kids;
Lost the job of course.
I didn't care to be honest,
Didn't seem to care about anything.
It was like I dried up inside.

Then one afternoon
I was walking in this bit of garden
They have out the back
And heard someone laughing in the greenhouse.
My dad was standing there all tears
Leaning on the water butt
This insect sprayer in his hand.
His cap had fallen on the floor.
He put his arms around me
And I felt his tears all down my neck.
I felt that terrible.
I thought, if my old dad
Can cry for me like that,
I must have been some use
To someone once upon a time.
The next day I went
And started circling likely jobs in red.

And now I'm here.
A new woman.
No I'll get these.
You haven't said much.
You're not the quiet type, are you?
I hope you're not deep.
Oh, that's good,
I don't trust people who're deep.
Can I ask you something?
D'you mind?
No, it's just that I was wondering,
What's your favourite Bros record?

Life as a Sheep

Sometimes
Oi stands
Sometimes
Oi sits
Then stands again
Then
Sits
For a bit.

Sometimes
Oi wanders
Sometimes
Oi stays
Sometimes
Oi chews
Sometimes
Oi strays.

Sometimes
Oi coughs
Sometimes
Oi don't
Sometimes
Oi bleats
Sometimes
Oi won't.

Sometimes
Oi watch
The human race
Or
Smiles to meself
Or
Stares into space.

And when Oi's 'appy
Oi'd dance and sing
But Oi don't have the knack
To do such a thing.

At night
Oi lays
By the old church steeple
And
Falls asleep
By counting people.

Printed in Great Britain
by Amazon.co.uk, Ltd.,
Marston Gate.